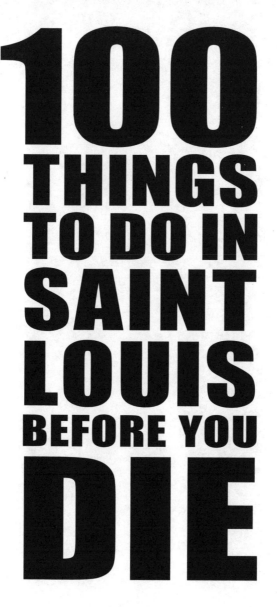

100 THINGS TO DO IN SAINT LOUIS BEFORE YOU DIE

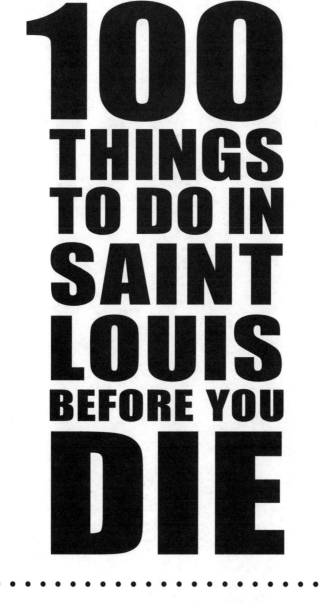

100 THINGS TO DO IN SAINT LOUIS BEFORE YOU DIE

AMANDA E. DOYLE

REEDY PRESS
St. Louis, Missouri

To Brian and Milo,
always at the top of my list

Reedy Press
PO Box 5131
St. Louis, MO 63139, USA
www.reedypress.com

Library of Congress Control Number: 2013938453

ISBN: 978-1-935806-50-9

Design by Jill Halpin

Printed in the United States of America
13 14 15 16 17   5 4 3 2 1

Please note that websites, phone numbers, addresses, and company names are subject to change or cancellation. We did our best to relay the most accurate information available, but due to circumstances beyond our control, please do not hold us liable for misinformation. When exploring new destinations, please do your homework before you go.

For more information, upcoming author events, and booksignings, please visit www.facebook.com/100ThingsSTL.

CONTENTS

xiii • Preface

3 • Beer Me at Anheuser-Busch

4 • Go Arch Raving Mad for the Missouri Valley Conference

5 • Sled Art Hill

6 • Think Big Thoughts at the Assembly Series

7 • Bask in the Glow

8 • Sing the Blues at BB's

9 • Commune with the Forebears at Bellefontaine Cemetery

10 • Chuck Berry Concert at Blueberry Hill

11 • Double Down on Fall Fun

12 • Hurt So Good at Bluesweek

14 • Paddle Around the Park

15 • Experience Beer-vana at the Saint Louis Brewers Heritage Festival

16 • Get Behind the Scenes at Busch Stadium

17 • Celebrate Solstice at Cahokia Mounds

19 • Stroll Down Candy Cane Lane

20 • Relive St. Louis's Victorian Heyday at the Campbell House

21 • Jump, Jive, Wail, and Swing at Casa Loma

23 • Play (on) the Ponies at Faust Park

24 • Experience Holy Awe at the Basilica

26 • Explore Central Library

27 • Live La Vida Cherokee

28 • Play Like a King at the St. Louis Chess Club

29 • Taste the Sawdust at Circus Flora

30 • Take a Spin on the Rooftop Ferris Wheel

31 • Splashing and Strolling at Citygarden

32 • Get Sousa-fied with the Compton Heights Concert Band

33 • Get High at the Compton Hill Water Tower

34 • Convene at the Confluence

35 • Set Sail on Creve Coeur Lake

36 • Suck Down a Malt at Crown Candy

37 • Mangia and Market on the Hill

38 • Get Your Irish Up at St. Patrick's Day Parade

41 • Treat Yourself at a Donut Shop

42 • Watch the Eagles Soar

43 • Eat a Slinger at Eat-Rite

44 • Pick Apples at Eckert's

45 • Hit the Hay at Faust Park

46 • Travel the Globe at Festival of Nations

47 • Take a Float Trip

48 • Lenten Fish Fry

51 • Taste the Frozen Rainbow

52 • Go to the Top in the Gateway Arch

53 • Push Pedals at the Gateway Cup

54 • Get Your Goat at Grant's Farm

57 • Fall for the Great River Road

58 • Explore Missouri's Black History

59 • Do the Twist at Gus'

60 • Trick or Treat the CWE

61 • Get Jazzy at the Bistro

62 • Dinner on the Hill

65 • Japanese Festival at Missouri Botanical Gardens

66 • March into History at Jefferson Barracks

67 • Spend Thursday Night at a Sneakeasy

68 • Remember Ragtime at Scott Joplin's House

71 • Acknowledge Mom's Artful Parenting at Laumeier

72 • Spook Yourself at Lemp Mansion

73 • Laugh at Old Man Winter in the Loop

74 • Find That One Elk

76 • Rock Out at LouFest

77 • Seek Out the Classic Magic

78 • Stroll the Cobblestones in Historic
St. Charles

79 • Fetch Some Fun at Mardi Gras

80 • Parade with a Purpose for Annie Malone

81 • Play Bocce Ball on the Hill

83 • Unearth Recent Missouri History

84 • Drink Missouri Wine

86 • Ride On at the Moonlight Ramble

87 • Celebrate the Season at the Old Courthouse

89 • Get Moving at the Museum of
Transportation

90 • Get Underground on a Cave Tour

91 • Go Bird-Watching on Opening Day

92 • Get Starstruck at the Planetarium

93 • Know Your River

94 • Na Zdrowie!

96 • Experience Pumpkinland

97 • Faire Thee Well at the St. Louis
Renaissance Faire

98 • Watch Spring Explode at Purina Farms

100 • Cruise the River

101 • Watch the World at the St. Louis
International Film Fest

103 • Bike the Riverfront Trail

104 • Eat Lebanese with the Lord

105 • Roll Thunder, Old-School at Saratoga

106 • Let the Music Play at Powell Hall

108 • Hike the Glades at Shaw Nature Reserve

109 • See a Show at the Sheldon

111 • Take Your Mama for Some Drama at the
Shakespeare Festival

112 • Swoon for a Summer Night

113 • Shop the Stalls of Soulard Market

114 • Settle a Grudge Match at South Broadway
Athletic Club

115 • Take a Twirl at Steinberg Rink

116 • Fill Up the Market Basket

119 • Revel in Rivalry on Turkey Day

120 • Share a Secret at Union Station

121 • Chill Out at Venice Café

122 • Get Up on the Roof at Vin de Set

123 • Dig Up New Tunes at Vintage Vinyl

124 • All Aboard! Wabash Frisco and Pacific Railroad

125 • Channel Your Inner Architect

126 • Wednesday Evening Concerts in the Whitaker Music Festival at Missouri Botanical Garden

128 • Waddle the Zoo

129 • Suggested Itineraries

132 • Activities by Season

134 • Index

PREFACE

Let's get one thing clear: Despite the title, even despite the cheeky bucket image on the cover, I'm not anxious for you to shuffle off this mortal coil anytime soon. For one thing, that would take you out of the book-buying market, and what author wants her audience to shrink?

While thinking about this book, this primer on St. Louis, I wanted to capture two realities: the urgency that I feel, because there are so many fantastically interesting corners of this town that enough people haven't yet explored, and the nagging certainty that I won't get to all of them, even though doing just that is both my profession and my avocation. In the comings and goings of work, family, and to-do lists of the mundane and the sometimes important, it's natural and easy to settle into a rut of familiarity. You *mean* to take the kids to Citygarden, or to check out the new restaurant, or to get those Chuck Berry tickets, but you just never do.

So here it is, in one handy format: a St. Louis bucket list. Notice, it's not "the best 100 places in St. Louis" or even "100 things you *must* do to be a legit St. Louisan"—who'd have the omniscience to know that? Those lists would depend entirely on too many moving and changeable factors.

No, this list offers a modest proposal. Here are 100 things that, should you take the time to experience them all, will give you a rounded St. Louis education, a great start on piecing together the puzzle of this magnificent city, an appreciation for what we have. Plunge right in from A to Z, hop around within the pages, or, if you like guidance, check out the Suggested Itineraries in the back of the book. Join other readers on Facebook (100ThingsSTL) to report back on what you discover. Let me know what else would make *your* list!

And just to be on the safe side, I'm making a point to leave an item or two unchecked, so I'll have a reason to hang around for a while longer.

Amanda E. Doyle
April 2013

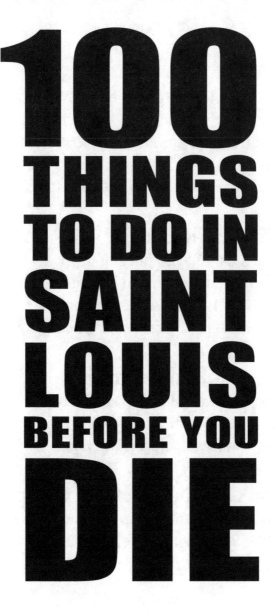

100 THINGS TO DO IN SAINT LOUIS BEFORE YOU DIE

So over the world's largest brewer? Well, you're in the right city for that, too. With at least twenty craft breweries fully operational, it's the perfect time to branch out and sample the microbrew taps. A few recommendations to get you started:

The Civil Life Brewing Co.
among the most relaxed pubs in town, also offering gourmet snacks and an in-house library
3714 Holt Ave., cash only
www.thecivillifebrewingcompany.com

4 Hands Brewing
big, bold, flavorful beers, and tasty food, too
1220 S. 8th St., 314-436-1559
www.4handsbrewery.com

Urban Chestnut Brewing Company
one of the prettiest beer gardens in town
3229 Washington Ave., 314-222-0143
www.urbanchestnut.com

BEER ME
AT ANHEUSER-BUSCH

Been on the free Anheuser-Busch tour? If not, do that first. OK, now we're all caught up and ready for the premium experience. For $25, upgrade to the Beermaster Tour, which takes aficionados into the fermentation cellars, the historic Brew House, the Clydesdale Stable & Tack Room, a packaging/bottling line, and private VIP tasting room, post-tour. You'll also get some nifty A-B swag to take home, along with a certificate of Beermaster completion, suitable for framing and hanging next to any other earned diplomas on your wall. And while you're encouraged to know your limits, it's worth mentioning the free tastings at the end are unlimited, and the tour itself includes a chug of beer straight out of one of the stainless steel finishing tanks.

1 Busch Place, www.anheuser-busch.com

GO ARCH RAVING MAD
FOR THE MISSOURI VALLEY CONFERENCE

Generally speaking, the attendees at the Arch Madness men's basketball tournament come from outside St. Louis, with fan bases that travel en masse from easy drive-in towns like Carbondale, Wichita, and Des Moines. Sports-savvy locals, though, know that the event has everything you'd want in a college tourney: competing bands, galloping mascots, face-painted cheerleaders, alumni living and dying with every shot. The basketball played in the Missouri Valley Conference has long been underrated, though their annual crowning of a league champ reminds you that the ball played in the Valley is high-quality hoops, indeed, with worthy theater in the stands and on the sidelines. A rooting interest is preferred, but not essential.

First weekend in March, Scottrade Center, 314-444-4300,
www.archmadness.com

SLED ART HILL

It's so iconic you might think it's overplayed, but the wide, gentle slope down to the Grand Basin from the Saint Louis Art Museum is the kind of hill sleds, saucers, and even cafeteria trays were born to glide. Sure, you'll have to cruise for parking, and yes, you'll need to pack your own hot chocolate. Shiny red cheeks and the pictures you'll get, to say nothing of some winter exercise, will be worth it.

In Forest Park

THINK BIG THOUGHTS
AT THE ASSEMBLY SERIES

The presence of several high-quality universities in St. Louis means a wealth of opportunities that can enrich the entire community . . . but only if the community finds out and takes advantage! Prime example? The Assembly Series of speakers at Washington University. For more than half a century, the school has organized lectures from well-known and highly regarded thinkers, writers, artists, and other influential folks to offer programs, free and open to the public, on some of the day's most important issues. From scientists to documentary filmmakers, from musicians to agents of historical change, it's an education you'd do well to acquire. Bonus: Frequently the lectures are held at the lovely Graham Chapel, as inspirational a setting as you'd hope to enjoy.

One Brookings Dr., 314-935-4620, assemblyseries.wustl.edu

BASK IN THE GLOW

The night before September's Great Forest Park Balloon Race, which just celebrated its fortieth anniversary, sees the park filled to the gills with families crowding in for the balloon glow, when you can get up close and personal to the tethered behemoths, inflated and lit by their burners. Stick around till the end and be treated to a fireworks extravaganza.

In Forest Park, Central Field, www.greatforestparkballoonrace.com

SING THE BLUES
AT BB'S

Live music. Every. Single. Night. Not many spots can make that claim, but BB's Jazz, Blues and Soups lives it, and ups the ante by using their stage and excellent sightlines (to say nothing of the lip-smacking, down-home food) to showcase the very best in homegrown jazz and blues talent. The occasional big-name touring show blows through, too, but nurturing a serious St. Louis scene is their cornbread and butter.

700 S. Broadway, 314-436-5222, www.bbsjazzbluessoups.com

COMMUNE WITH THE FOREBEARS
AT BELLEFONTAINE CEMETERY

The powers that be at Bellefontaine Cemetery know that sedate and stodgy isn't going to get them anywhere. They'd prefer you come and see the resting places of some of the folks—famous, infamous, and everything in between—who put St. Louis on the map. Monthly second-Saturday tours, along with special themed tours including "Beer Barons" and "Women of Note," will reveal the sometimes-spectacular permanent residences of folks from Adolphus Busch to Sara Teasdale.

Nestled next door to Bellefontaine is the Catholic counterpart, Calvary Cemetery, where the final resting places of prominent people include René Auguste Chouteau, William Tecumseh Sherman, Tennessee Williams, Kate Chopin, and Dred Scott. Let the history lessons begin.

Bellefontaine:
4947 W. Florissant Ave., 314-381-0750, bellefontainecemetery.org

Calvary:
5239 W. Florissant Ave., 314-792-7738,
archstl.org/cemeteries/content/view/91/233/

8

CHUCK BERRY
CONCERT
AT BLUEBERRY HILL

Our homegrown international rock 'n roll sensation is on the far side of eighty . . . you don't have forever. Pick a month, get your tickets early, and appreciate the genius that endures.

6504 Delmar Blvd., 314-727-4444,
www.blueberryhill.com

DOUBLE DOWN
ON FALL FUN

They're smart, these city dwellers. By putting on the Best of
Missouri Market (at the Missouri Botanical Garden) and
the Historic Shaw Art Fair (across the street in the Shaw
neighborhood) on the same fall-licious weekend, they figured
they'd capitalize on all the handcrafted, local art, and artisan-
loving folks who'd naturally be drawn to either event on its own.
The result? At least a weekend's worth of exceptional art, craft,
furniture, foodstuffs, and entertainment, no matter how you split
your days. Special shout-out here to the cow-milking station at
the Best of Missouri Market: That's a can't-miss photo op.

First full weekend of October

Missouri Botanical Garden:
4344 Shaw Blvd., 314-577-5100,
www.missouribotanicalgarden.org

Historic Shaw Art Fair:
4100 and 4200 blocks of Flora Place, 314-773-3101,
www.shawartfair.org

HURT SO GOOD
AT BLUESWEEK

This river city has a long and complex history with America's music, the blues; unfortunately, it's taken us a long time to understand the importance of that history and get a proper understanding and celebration going for it. One great way to educate and enjoy yourself simultaneously is at the St. Louis Bluesweek Festival, at Soldiers Memorial. Famous acts, players, and singers who have been there and back share the stage with some of the most promising and prominent St. Louis blues musicians. Admission is free, but if you care to make a $5 donation at the door, it'll go towards the construction of the National Blues Museum taking shape downtown.

Memorial Day Weekend, 1315 Chestnut St., 314-534-2100, www.bluesweek.com

Tip:

Come hungry! The BBQ Battle Royale during the event pits thirty teams against each other for bragging rights of "the best Q in the Lou."

PADDLE
AROUND THE PARK

Cast off, at least temporarily, from the bustle of Forest Park in a paddleboat built for two, three, or four. You might surprise yourself with how far you can get through the interconnected system of lakes and lagoons, and it won't take long before you can easily spot herons, sunning turtles, and curious ducks. When your legs give out, steam back into port and enjoy lunch or a drink dockside at the Boat House, where those same curious ducks can get downright grabby when it comes to the last French fry.

6101 Government Dr., 314-367-2224, www.boathouseforestpark.com

EXPERIENCE BEER-VANA
AT THE SAINT LOUIS BREWERS HERITAGE FESTIVAL

Roam free under the giant tents with more than eighty beers, produced by around twenty of the finest local and craft brewers, that are yours for the sampling. From stalwarts to experimental new recipes, you'll get to try ales, lagers, hybrids, and homebrews in a beer-garden-party atmosphere. Live musical entertainment and food from several local vendors makes for a full afternoon or evening session, and the proceeds benefit Lift for Life, a nonprofit providing safe and nurturing after-school programs for kids.

GET BEHIND THE SCENES
AT BUSCH STADIUM

While you're waiting to get called up to the majors, there's an easier way to experience the ambience from a big-league dugout. Daily tours—except on home-day game dates—strike out from the Stan Musial statue and take fans to the Cardinals dugout, the Champions Club (home of the World Series trophies), and even the radio broadcast booth, where you can practice your own play-by-play. Make the call.

700 Clark St., 314-345-9565, www.cardinals.com

CELEBRATE SOLSTICE
AT CAHOKIA MOUNDS

Our very own backyard (well, Southern Illinois, anyway) boasts a UNESCO World Heritage Site—meaning if you haven't made it to the prehistoric metropolis of Cahokia Mounds, it's like skipping out on the Great Wall of China, or the Taj Mahal. For what, so you could sleep in? Set the alarm and hightail it to the summer—or winter—solstice celebration atop 100-foot-high Monk's Mound, to welcome the dawn with a small-but-hardy bunch of your fellow homo sapiens.

30 Ramey St., Collinsville, IL, 618-346-5160, cahokiamounds.org

Tip:

Rather than idling in the sometimes-long car line, park around the corner and bundle up for a winter stroll down the block.

STROLL DOWN
CANDY CANE LANE

Not a creation of Willie Wonka, but an actual residential street in the St. Louis Hills neighborhood, the 6500 block of Murdoch transforms itself, via thousands of lights and countless hours of neighbor-labor, into a twinkling wonderland of Christmas cheer. For about a decade, the residents here have been inviting visitors in, and collecting voluntary donations for area charities. They've been so successful that adjacent blocks have joined in the fun, too.

6500 block of Murdoch Ave., St. Louis Hills

Other wonderland streets in the neighborhood:

Angel Avenue: 4700 block of Prague Ave.
Snow Flake Street: 6500 block of Neosho St.

RELIVE ST. LOUIS'S VICTORIAN HEYDAY
AT THE CAMPBELL HOUSE

An afternoon at downtown's Campbell House steeps you in the culture and trappings of the 1880s, through the remarkably restored mansion (built in 1851) of Robert Campbell, a rough-and-tumble frontier fur trader who traded in that life (mostly) to become a pillar of civilized society. The home contains hundreds of original possessions, furnishings, artwork, letters, and more belonging to the family and shows a city growing into its role in a young, optimistic country.

1508 Locust St., 314-421-0325, www.campbellhousemuseum.org

JUMP, JIVE, WAIL, AND SWING
AT CASA LOMA

Learn how to do any of the above at the Casa Loma Ballroom, a staple just off Cherokee Street that's been home to folks wanting to shake a tail-feather since the mid-1930s. Big bands and rockers still grace the stage, with ballroom Fridays and swing Saturdays proving to be steady draws. Lessons often precede the full evening's dance card.

3354 Iowa Ave., 314-664-8000, www.casalomaballroom.com

Tip:

If it happens to be March, nothing fights the gloom of those last winter days like the thousands of vibrant, near-metallic Blue Morpho peleides butterflies that fill the Butterfly House next door to the Carousel during March Morpho Mania, daily from 9 a.m. to 4 p.m. all month long.

PLAY (ON) THE PONIES
AT FAUST PARK

Or the reindeer, or winged griffin-esque creatures . . . at the St. Louis Carousel. Kids and adults can experience the real deal on the circa-1920 merry-go-round, relocated here from its beloved original location at the Forest Park Highlands Amusement Park. Vigorous musical accompaniment by the Stinson Band Organ makes the $2/spin a great deal. Worth a mention is the unusual carousel- and music-box-themed gift shop.

In Faust Park, 15189 Olive Blvd., 314-615-8383,
www.stlouisco.com/ParksandRecreation/ParkPages/Faust

EXPERIENCE HOLY AWE
AT THE BASILICA

Awe is the natural reaction in the remarkable presence of the world's largest collection of mosaic art under one (big) roof, at the Cathedral Basilica. Walls and ceilings tell stories of Christ, Catholicism, and the affairs of the Church and its mission in the local area. A fascinating mosaic museum in the basement demonstrates the marriage of artistry and precision required to make the vision a reality.

4431 Lindell Blvd., 314-373-8241, www.cathedralstl.org

Tip:

If you want an expert to show you the highlights, call ahead for a tour reservation, available weekdays from 10 a.m. to 4 p.m. Sunday tours, following noon Mass, don't need a reservation.

EXPLORE
CENTRAL LIBRARY

Following a meticulous $70 million renovation that touched on everything from interior lights to relocating literally tons of volumes, the flagship downtown branch of the St. Louis Public Library wows anew with soaring public spaces, an inviting and interactive kids' wing, the inspiring "St. Louis Room," a main-floor café, spiffy new auditorium space (where the coal bin once lived), and much more. This ain't your grandpa's library . . . but bring him along for the fun! And it's not just local boosters who have noticed the spiffy restoration. In early 2013, the reborn library won the popular vote in the Architizer A+ Library Award, an international competition.

1301 Olive St., 314-241-2288, www.slpl.org

LIVE LA VIDA CHEROKEE

One of the most consistently interesting mashups in town occurs along the length of Cherokee Street, on the city's South Side. A Mexican/Latin American business district offers everything from authentic beef tongue tacos to jerseys from the world's best soccer teams, while artists and cultural creatives have brought everything from letterpress printing and neighborhood-niche T-shirts to handmade art jewelry and hard-to-find music. Spend some time to find your own favorites. Stumped? Start at: La Vallesana, Apop, Stylehouse, St. Louis Curio Shoppe, Flowers to the People, Siete Luminarias, I Scream Cakes, Gooolll, The Firecracker Press, or Mo Moderne.

www.cherokeestation.com

PLAY LIKE A KING
AT THE ST. LOUIS CHESS CLUB

Ever since philanthropist Rex Sinquefield decided to make it
so, St. Louis has evolved into an international hub for chess.
Across Maryland Avenue from each other in the Central West
End, the World Chess Hall of Fame and the Chess Club and
Scholastic Center of St. Louis form the epicenter. Hit up the Hall
for changing exhibits related to chess, art, and other intersecting
topics, and a terrific gift shop. Want to learn the basics of the
game of kings, or looking for a place where there's always
someone willing to set up across the board? A membership at
the Chess Club is all you'll need, and you'll get facetime with
some of the game's visiting luminaries, too.

Chess Club:
4657 Maryland Ave., 314-361-2437,
www.saintlouischessclub.org

Hall of Fame:
4652 Maryland Ave., 314-367-9243,
www.worldchesshof.org

TASTE THE SAWDUST
AT CIRCUS FLORA

It's worth starting a summer circus tradition with your own family, and there's no better place than at the charming, one-ring wonder under a classic red-and-white-striped big top in Grand Center. For nearly a month, the parking lot behind Powell Hall is overtaken by high-wire daredevils, aerialists, jugglers, acrobats, fast-paced and funny animal acts, and one irrepressible clown, Nino. You can sit close enough to taste the sawdust, if that's your thing; live music makes the experience even more magical.

Grand Blvd. and Samuel Shepard Dr., 314-289-4040, www.circusflora.org

TAKE A SPIN
ON THE ROOFTOP FERRIS WHEEL

There's run-of-the-mill wacky, and then there's City Museum–grade wacky. The fantastical, industrial, recycled playspace that was the brainchild of artist Bob Cassilly achieves its apex, appropriately, up on the roof. A schoolbus dangles off one corner, appearing to lurch precariously off the building, and slides of varying levels of potential danger are scattered about. But you're already this high, so why not add four more stories to it? Stand in line to ride Big Eli, the restored Ferris wheel that, in temperate months, takes you up to an unparalleled view of the city.

701 N. 15th St., 314-231-CITY, www.citymuseum.org

SPLASHING AND STROLLING
AT CITYGARDEN

The ultimate "build it, and they will come" project, this interactive sculpture park and water-filled oasis smack dab in the heart of downtown brings together wading kids, sun-seeking escapees from the nearby office high-rises, curious out-of-towners, and the rest of life's rich pageant. Wander among the giant bunnies, sideways head, bird-boy hybrid, and lots of other playful art, while the anxious-looking security guards try to decide how much to rein in the exuberance. BYO sunscreen and blanket, but if you forget the picnic, well-stocked food trucks tend to congregate nearby.

8th, 9th, and 10th Sts., between Market and Chestnut Sts.,
www.citygardenstl.org

GET SOUSA-FIED
WITH THE COMPTON HEIGHTS
CONCERT BAND

Old-fashioned (and free!) family entertainment—in the form of marches, show tunes, and singalongs—is enthusiastically delivered by this community ensemble and their frequent guest artists—everyone from Mariachi Los Camperos de Nati Cano to the late Stan Musial, who was an amateur harmonicist. Sunday Serenades in Francis Park and Musical Mondays in Tower Grove Park happen June to August, 7:30 p.m. Arrive earlier than that for a good view.

Francis Park:
St. Louis Hills neighborhood; bounded by Tamm, Eichelberger, Nottingham, and Donovan

Tower Grove Park:
Bounded by Magnolia, Grand, Arsenal, and Kingshighway

GET HIGH
AT THE COMPTON HILL WATER TOWER

One hundred and ninety-eight steps, and you'll find yourself at the top of the 170-foot French Romanesque Compton Hill Water Tower, as elegant a shell as was ever constructed to conceal a 100-foot standpipe. Built in 1898, the tower offers 360-degree views as far as Illinois and the Jefferson Barracks Bridge. It is open the first Saturday of each month from April to November, from noon to 4 p.m., as well as on the evenings of full moons during those months.

In Compton Hill Reservoir Park,
Grand & Russell Blvds., 314-552-9000,
www.watertowerfoundation.org

CONVENE
AT THE CONFLUENCE

Where the Mississippi and Missouri rivers swirl together, some of the wildest, widest swaths in the region offer a dizzying array of opportunities to observe, to commune with, and to learn about the natural world. An excellent starting place is the Visitor Center at the Columbia Bottom Conservation Area, the doorway to more than 4,300 acres of trails, marshy wetlands, prairies, bottomland hardwoods, and other native habitats. This is heaven for birders.

I-270 north to Riverview Dr., then north about 2.5 miles, 314-877-6014, mdc.mo.gov

SET SAIL
ON CREVE COEUR LAKE

Ahoy, landlocked landlubbers! You don't need open water to earn your skipper's bragging rights. Head out to Creve Coeur Lake on alternate Sundays (check the online calendar) for small sailboat races. The action starts late morning, when the sailors arrive with their boats and begin setting up sails and rigging. Novices are more than welcome to lend a helping set of hands, and you may find yourself on the water as a volunteer crew member.

Marine Ave., near Dorsett Rd., 314-576-7200, www.sailccsa.com

SUCK DOWN A MALT
AT CROWN CANDY

Pretty much every celebrity chef with a TV show has tried it, and they're not better than you! Whether you aim for Crown Candy Kitchen's five-malt challenge or just want to conquer one, your tastebuds will thank you. You can always wash it down with a BLT.

1401 St. Louis Ave., 314-621-9650, www.crowncandykitchen.net

For a similar-but-different dining experience in the mid-county area, find a seat at Carl's Drive-In, where the milkshakes come in two flavors (chocolate and vanilla), the root-beer float features housemade soda, and your bill will need to be settled up in cash.
9033 Manchester Rd., 314-961-9652

MANGIA AND MARKET
ON THE HILL

On the Hill, of course, you can, and should, eat Italian food (see Dinner on the Hill, page 62, for my picks.) You can also shop like an Italian, stocking up on essentials from imported tomatoes and more pasta shapes than you might've known existed to hard candies, St. Louis–style pizza fixings, house-cured meats, deli sandwiches, specialty flours and sauces, Italian-themed gifts, kitchen gadgets, and so much more. All products are priced reasonably, even when compared to the big guys! Of several worthy options, the nod here goes to DiGregorio's Market, a clean, well-lighted space where it's nearly impossible to leave empty-handed.

5200 Daggett Ave., 314-776-1062, www.digregoriofoods.com

GET YOUR IRISH UP
AT ST. PATRICK'S DAY PARADE

One of the several proud waves of immigrants who came early and plentifully to these Mississippi shores, the Irish (and would-be Irish) of St. Louis maintain a lively presence felt most keenly around St. Patrick's Day, when both a proper downtown parade and a neighborhood-based celebration draw crowds. Get the most authentic flavor at the Dogtown parade, held on the day itself down Tamm Avenue, workdays and weekdays be damned. From floats bearing dancers to families and friends marching under their clan's heritage crest, it's a family-friendly (if a bit raucous) good time.

Tip:

Following the lead of Mardi Gras, no coolers are allowed into the neighborhood on parade day. Save yourself time and possible ticketing and park in the Zoo's south lot. You can easily get to the parade by walking over the Tamm bridge to Dogtown. Join the hardy crowd for pre-parade breakfast at Pat's Bar & Grill.

Donut Drive-In
6525 Chippewa St., 314-645-7714

O'Fashion
5120 Southwest Ave., 314-772-0398

Eddie's
4701 S. Kingshighway Blvd., 314-832-1200

Duke Bakery
819 Henry St., Alton, IL, 618-462-2922,
www.dukebakeryinc.com

World's Fair
904 Vandeventer Ave., 314-776-9975

Strange Donuts
2709 Sutton Blvd., 314-398-9530,
www.strangedonuts.com

TREAT YOURSELF
AT A DONUT SHOP

This is a family donut shop town, and you'll have a time keeping your BMI down if you survey all the "bests" that neighbors and co-workers will recommend. From the Donut Drive-In (where people wait in line, because they're just that good) to O'Fashion (where numerous images of the King smile down beatifically at your selection, thankyuhverymuch), from Eddie's Southtown Donuts (where patrons seem to enjoy the namesake's swagger almost as much as they enjoy his delectable donuts) to the way-old-school glazed goodies at Duke Bakery in Alton, Illinois, well—there's just no excuse to eat chain donuts unless you have to. We're partial to the whole experience at World's Fair Donuts. Peggy (she of the gravity-defying bouffant and quick-as-a-wink mental addition) will keep your order straight in her head, grabbing your fried pie or chocolate long john, milk, or coffee. She'll whip up your total with a stubby pencil while, behind her, husband Terry and son Byron crank out the next batch of dough, something they do seven days a week at the shop started in the 1940s by Terry's father. Most of these shops are cash-only.

For something completely different, check out Strange Donuts in Maplewood: maple and bacon glaze, Captain Crunch cereal-encrusted donuts, and many more.

WATCH
THE EAGLES SOAR

Winter's no time for dedicated naturalists to stay indoors; not with the mass migration overhead of flocks of bald eagles heading south along the Mississippi corridor. Some terrific spots to see them include the Old Chain of Rocks Bridge or the Audubon Center at Riverlands, a birders paradise featuring an educational/interpretive center and outdoor viewing opportunities.

301 Riverlands Way, West Alton, 636-899-0090,
riverlands.audubon.org

EAT A SLINGER
AT EAT-RITE

Like Protestant denominations, the details may vary slightly, but most agree: pile a mess of hash browns, breakfast meat, eggs, chili, cheese, and onions on a plate, and you've got yourself a delicacy. It ain't fancy, ergo neither should your surroundings be. Get yours with a side of 'tude at Eat-Rite Diner.

622 Chouteau Ave., 314-621-9621, you're seriously looking for a website?

Other slingers of note around town:
Big Ed's Chili Mac's Diner, downtown, is a classic
in part because of its delicious homemade chili,
510 Pine St., 314-421-9040.
White Knight Diner, a.k.a. where the movie *White Palace* was
filmed, slings a worthy variation, 1801 Olive St., 314-621-5949.
Local Harvest Café, for the twist: the vegan slinger, which
includes roasted local potato hash and their homemade vegan
chili, 3137 Morgan Ford Rd., 314-772-8815,
www.localharvestcafe.com.

PICK APPLES
AT ECKERT'S

What could be more wholesome? Head for the mother ship—and add on a hayride, mini-golf, push-pedal tractors, petting zoo, and more—at Eckert's Belleville Farm. In addition to the field and farm fun, there's an enormous market featuring their own produce and great finds from baked goods to jams, specialty candies to teas, and much more. Of course, all that fresh country air will probably work up your appetite, so plop down at the country restaurant for a hearty meal, but save room for a stop at the custard stand for dessert. And if it's not apple season? Not to worry. There are u-pick schedules for blackberries, peaches, and pumpkins, too, along with cut-your-own Christmas trees.

951 S. Green Mount Rd., IL, 618-233-0513, www.eckerts.com

HIT THE HAY
AT FAUST PARK

Clamber on up to the flatbed trailer and stake your spot on a hay bale for a fall ride through Faust Park, which includes a stop or two for schooling on the park's historic significance. Then clamber back down and spend a few minutes or hours exploring the candlelit village's restored buildings. A working blacksmith shop, a re-enacted prairie funeral, and a one-room schoolhouse are among the highlights. Period-authentic refreshments are served, and ample entertainment is provided by the live folk music and raging bonfires. Advance reservations required.

15185 Olive Blvd., 314-615-8328,
www.stlouisco.com/ParksandRecreation/ParkPages/Faust

TRAVEL THE GLOBE
AT FESTIVAL OF NATIONS

And eat all its foods. It's kind of cliché to say that many people save up calories all year just to chow down on the amazing international cuisines available at the weekend-long Festival of Nations, but there are so many tempting treats that it's hard not to want to binge. Step away from the fry bread, kebabs, and samosas for a few moments, and you'll find the cultural offerings pretty filling, too: music, dance, crafts, cultural demonstrations, merchandise, games, and so much more.

Late August, in Tower Grove Park, 2710 S. Grand Blvd., 314-773-9090, www.festivalofnationsstl.org

TAKE A FLOAT TRIP

Choose your speed: steady and sporty (canoe), punctuated equilibrium (rafting), slow and meandering (inner tube). Choose your spot: Current, Jacks Fork, Black, Huzzah, and Meramec rivers are among the best nearby. Choose your day: weekdays for smaller crowds/fewer hoosiers, weekends for the full party. All that's left now is to pack your cooler and sunscreen and hit the water.

Among the outfitters:
Akers Ferry: 573-858-3224, www.currentrivercanoe.com

Forest 44 Canoe Rental: 314-255-7091, www.forest44canoerental.com

Bearcat Getaway: 573-637-2264, www.bearcatgetaway.com

LENTEN FISH FRY

You're Catholic, and Fridays during Lent are the time to observe the spirit of sacrifice. You're Catholic, and you don't really go in for all that dogma, but you still have to support your parish. You're not Catholic, but you live in a fairly Catholic city, the spirit of community will warm your heart, and hey, you gotta eat! Pack up the kids (they're more than welcome), about $20, and prepare to feast like royalty. Three picks: St. Cecilia Parish, home of the outrageously popular (read: long line) Mexican fish fry, with fish, tacos, chiles rellenos, and a mariachi band; St. Peter Parish, appropriately enough in St. Peters, filling out the menu with frog legs, peel-and-eat shrimp, and baked potatoes; and St. Pius V, who serve on china, have great live music, and boast some of the most helpful table-clearing kids on the South Side.

St. Cecilia
5418 Louisiana Ave.,
314-351-1318,
www.stceciliaparishstl.org

St. Peter
221 First Capitol Dr.,
636-946-6641,
www.saintpeterchurchandschool.org

St. Pius V
3310 S. Grand Blvd.,
314-772-1525,
www.stpiusv.org

Ted Drewes

6726 Chippewa St., 314-481-2652, and
4224 S. Grand Blvd. (open summer only),
314-352-7376,
www.teddrewes.com

Mr. Wizard's

2101 S. Big Bend Blvd., 314-781-7566,
www.wizardcustard.com

Fritz's

815 Meramec Station Rd., 636-225-8737,
www.fritzsfrozencustard.com

Annie's

245 S. Buchanan St., Edwardsville, IL, 618-656-0289,
www.anniesfrozencustard.com

Bobby's

2525 N. Center St., Maryville, IL, 618-345-3002,
www.bobbysfrozencustard.com

The Whistle Stop

1 Carson Rd., 314-521-1600,
www.whistlestopdepot.com

TASTE
THE FROZEN RAINBOW

You've got the grandaddy of frozen custard, Ted Drewes. But plenty of partisans prefer Mr. Wizard's or Fritz's. Annie's and Bobby's pack 'em in on the Illinois side. It's practically a civic requirement, in Ferguson, to hang out at the Whistle Stop. Seems there's only one fair way to decide on the best, and that's to sample them all.

42

GO TO THE TOP
IN THE GATEWAY ARCH

Seriously. Just go, already. You have my permission. You don't even need an out-of-towner.

St. Louis Riverfront, 877-982-1410, www.gatewayarch.com

PUSH PEDALS
AT THE GATEWAY CUP

Labor Day Weekend is not all pork steaks and putting away the summer whites: in Lafayette Square, Benton Park, the Hill, and St. Louis Hills, it's race time. The Gateway Cup series brings professional criterium cycling (that's bicycle racing, for the layperson) to some of the city's prettiest neighborhoods for some heart-pumping straightaways and turns. Kids get a shot at the action in timed races, by age group, on the courses before the pros—here from all over the country—take over. Plenty of neighbors and businesses along the course get into the fun by turning their front yards and walkways into party patios.

Labor Day Weekend, 314-645-1362, www.gatewaycup.com

GET YOUR GOAT
AT GRANT'S FARM

The goats at Grant's Farm have terrorized generations of St. Louis children; why should yours (or you) be any different? Watch as delight turns to abject horror when the wee ones enter the arena with milk bottles at the ready. These cloven-hooved bandits have no decency. Make no mistake: they'd as soon eat you as look at you. OK, probably not. But adult males, especially, should take care to protect themselves. Turns out some vital organs are right about head-butting level.

10501 Gravois Rd., 314-843-1700, www.grantsfarm.com

Tip:

Pony up a little more than $200 (for a group of twelve or fewer) and take the Grant's Farm Private Expedition. A private vehicle safari through Deer Park, with hand-feeding of animals and fish, and a visit to the Clydesdale stables are among the highlights. Call 314-525-0829 for scheduling info.

Tip:
The northern terminus of the Great River Road puts you at Pere Marquette State Park, a great spot for breakfast or lunch in its rustic lodge. You can also enjoy horseback trail riding and hiking in the park. www.pmlodge.net

❦

FALL
FOR THE GREAT RIVER ROAD

It's the Mississippi River as you may never have seen it before, all shimmery and glorious in its wildness, with the dramatic limestone bluffs of Alton, Elsah, and Grafton, Illinois, soaring up to its east. For fall foliage peeping, the drive can't be beat. Along the way, make sure to pay respect to the legendary painted Piasa bird just north of Alton. The fearsome man-eater first appeared in prehistoric pictographs and is no less menacing today.

Cross the river at the Clark Bridge at Alton, IL, www.greatriverroad.com

EXPLORE
MISSOURI'S BLACK HISTORY

From Africans brought across the Middle Passage during the slave trade to Dred and Harriet Scott, whose appeal for their freedom and rights shook the world, to Madame C. J. Walker, widely acknowledged as America's first self-made female millionaire, the influence of prominent and ordinary black citizens on our state—and indeed, on the world—is both profound and undersung. At The Griot Museum of Black History, visitors can build on their knowledge of important African-American historical figures through artifacts, wax figurines, and traveling exhibits. Special events and a shop add to the experience.

2505 St. Louis Ave., 314-241-7057, www.thegriotmuseum.com

DO THE TWIST
AT GUS'

At Gus' Pretzels, you can stick to the basics (stick pretzels or the iconic pretzel twist), but feel free to branch out if you're not wedded to tradition: brats, salsiccia, and hot dogs hand-rolled inside pretzels, or party pretzels shaped like baby carriages, the Arch, the Cardinals logo, and more. Bring cash.

1820 Arsenal St., 314-664-4010, www.guspretzels.com

TRICK OR TREAT
THE CWE

If you're not from these parts, you'll soon discover that Halloween is serious business in St. Louis. Many folks will actually expect their trick-or-treaters to come prepared with a joke or other payment for that candy, and as with many other formerly-reserved-for-kids phenomena, the grownups have horned in on the fun a bit. For a daylong observance of the holiday that candy built, hit the Central West End on the Saturday prior to Halloween: late morning, there's a children's parade and trick-or-treating throughout the neighborhood's streets, and after lunch, a costumed pet parade. Then after the kids hit the sugar-high wall and are tucked away with visions of cavities dancing in their heads, the same streets are taken over by costumed (and often, drunken) adults, competing for cash prizes in a costume contest and enjoying the food, drinks, and other hijinks offered by the local bars and restaurants.

Centered at the intersection of Maryland and Euclid Aves.,
www.thecwe.org/events/cwe-halloween

GET JAZZY
AT THE BISTRO

Turn off your phone and tame your table conversation: Folks come to Jazz at the Bistro to *hear the music*. If it's been a while since you enjoyed the phenomenon, the early and late sets here—featuring a wide variety of solid players, groups, and vocalists—will be a revelation. It's a reception that wows the performers, too, and they pay it back in spades with enthusiastic endorsements, musical and spoken, from the stage. Love jazz? You'll love this. Know nothing about jazz? You'll love this, too.

3536 Washington Ave., 314-289-4030, www.jazzstlouis.org

DINNER ON THE HILL

The Hill offers an almost can't-go-wrong collection of Italian restaurants. A grab bag of three: for the full-on fine-dining experience, Dominic's; for St. Louis Italian-American the way it was popularized, Zia's; for a sleeper hit, Lorenzo's Trattoria. Want to recreate a meal at home? Shop for authentic ingredients at DiGregorio's Market (see Mangia and Market, page 37).

The following streets border the Hill:
Manchester, Hampton, Kingshighway, Southwest, and Columbia

Dominic's
5101 Wilson Ave.,
314-771-1632,
www.dominicsrestaurant.com

Zia's
5256 Wilson Ave.,
314-776-0020,
www.zias.com

Lorenzo's Trattoria
1933 Edwards St.,
314-773-2223,
www.lorenzostrattoria.com

⚜

Tip:

Available spots (twenty per tour) for the teahouse tour are snapped up quickly, so send someone from your party to stand in line if that's one of your priorities. Tickets are $5 each (cash only, max of four per person), and sold twice daily at the Plum Viewing Arbor. Tickets go on sale one hour before the first scheduled tour of each daily set and are sold for all tours in that set. Check the website at festival time to find each day's set times.

JAPANESE FESTIVAL
AT MISSOURI BOTANICAL GARDENS

At more than thirty-five years old, this annual Labor Day Weekend gathering is one of the oldest in the United States devoted to exploring the history, culture, and people of Japan—a milestone that makes sense when you consider the special relationship the Missouri Botanical Garden has had with Japan since the dedication of its Japanese Garden, Seiwa-en, in 1977. From *ikebana* (the Japanese art of flower arranging) and impressive taiko drumming to exclusive Teahouse Island tours and tea ceremonies, the weekend is a kaleidoscope of sights, sounds, and experiences visitors won't soon forget.

Labor Day Weekend, 4344 Shaw Blvd., 314-577-5100,
www.missouribotanicalgarden.org

MARCH INTO HISTORY
AT JEFFERSON BARRACKS

During World War II Weekend, the public is invited to stroll the grounds of Jefferson Barracks Park, where re-enactors representing U.S., British, Canadian, Soviet, and German troops of the period are camped. The re-enactors educate visitors about their uniforms, weapons, and equipment. Battle re-enactments give an up-close and personal view of warfare of the period, and kids are allowed to gather spent shell casings as souvenirs after the smoke clears.

Last weekend of April, 345 North Rd., 314-615-5270, stlouisco.com/ParksandRecreation/ParkPages/JeffersonBarracks

Ages eighteen and up can enjoy a typical World War II "canteen dance" with a visiting Big Band on Saturday night. Brush up on your swing moves!

SPEND THURSDAY NIGHT
AT A SNEAKEASY

Sneakeasy. I just made up that word, but it's an attempt to capture the mix of cool and sly and secret and fun that pervades just about any and everything that goes down on a Thursday evening at Joe's Café & Gallery, two quasi-private spaces next door to each other in the Skinker-DeBaliviere neighborhood. And the best part? Any and everything pretty much describes what you might find. For starters: Thursday nights at the age thirty-plus space are BYOB (or not, depending on what mood the city excise commissioner is in at the moment) and usually feature a smokin' band onstage. Joe's often offers Styrofoam bowls of snacks at the bar or on café tables and always features the wildly eclectic décor you might expect from proprietor and artist Bill Christman. Next door, he curates fantastical gallery shows also open during the Thursday affairs. Outside, he has curated a whole different scene, with a tiki garden, giant heads, and industrial bric-a-brac. One of the city's most unusual, welcoming, and cool-kid scenes.

6014 Kingsbury Ave., 314-862-2541,
www.facebook.com/ArsPopuliGallery

REMEMBER RAGTIME
AT SCOTT JOPLIN'S HOUSE

Scott Joplin, the king of ragtime, spent some of his most productive years living with his wife in a second-floor flat in St. Louis where he wrote some of his most famous works, including "Elite Syncopations" and "The Entertainer." Today, it's preserved as the Scott Joplin House State Historic Site, and you'll hear his melodies on a player piano as you tour the home.

2658A Delmar Blvd., 314-340-5790,
www.mostateparks.com/scottjoplin.htm

Tip:

Want a modern-day ragtime experience? The Friends of Scott Joplin organization hosts a rollicking Ragtime Rendezvous at 5:30 p.m. the first Sunday of each month upstairs at Dressel's Pub, 419 N. Euclid Ave. in the Central West End. See www.friendsofscottjoplin.org for details.

Missed Mother's Day?

Several other high-quality art fairs are worth the browse. In Belleville, the annual Art on the Square fair happens the weekend after Mother's Day. The Saint Louis Art Fair, in Clayton, is a cherished annual tradition for many in September. And Art Outside, hosted by Schlafly Bottleworks, takes a different tack on the same September weekend, highlighting affordable art and crafts from exclusively local makers.

Art on the Square
800-677-9255, www.artonthesquare.com

Saint Louis Art Fair
314-863-0278, www.culturalfestivals.com

Art Outside
314-241-2337, ext. 252,
www.schlafly.com/events

ACKNOWLEDGE MOM'S ARTFUL PARENTING
AT LAUMEIER

Any mom worth her salt will do the denial thing: "No, no, don't get me anything for Mother's Day; I just want to sit at home surrounded by my loving kids all day." That's a load of bull, best expunged by the sunshine, fresh air, and truly lovely surroundings of the annual Mother's Day art fair at Laumeier Sculpture Park. Excellent curated fine art and crafts from around the nation, plus music and wine tasting, makes mom even happier than a nap. Well, at least as happy as a nap.

Mother's Day Weekend, 12580 Rott Rd., 314-615-5278,
www.laumeiersculpturepark.org

SPOOK YOURSELF
AT LEMP MANSION

The much-put-upon Lemp family of St. Louis brewing fame experienced more than its fair share of depression, suicide, and unexplained death. But misery loves entrepreneurship, and the folks at the Lemp Mansion have turned those frowns upside down with "the Lemp Experience," a ghost-hunting/supernatural investigatory tour of the property . . . plus drinks and appetizers. Add on an overnight stay to really scare your pants off.

3322 DeMenil Place, 314-664-8024, www.lempmansion.com

LAUGH AT
OLD MAN WINTER
IN THE LOOP

If you can't beat 'em, join 'em. Surely that was one reason bandied about at the creation of the Loop Ice Carnival, a January weekend of frozen-buns family fun, from ice sculpting and ice slides to fire jugglers and human dog sledders. Businesses up and down Delmar have snacks, special sales, and games, and the collection of zany you'll find here reminds you why the Loop is good for any reason, in every season.

www.visittheloop.com/about/events

FIND THAT
ONE ELK

In fact, at Lone Elk Park, you'll find him and plenty of his compatriots, along with bison, wild turkeys, deer, turtles, and more, with the more charismatic megafauna fairly likely to mosey up to your car to see if any snacks are in the offing.

1 Lone Elk Park Rd., 314-615-7275,
www.stlouisco.com/ParksandRecreation/ParkPages/LoneElk

While You're There:

You're right next door, so fly on over to the World Bird Sanctuary for a unique opportunity to see falcons, owls, hawks, eagles, and more wild birds, in habitat displays and seriously up-close encounters. No charge for either park.

ROCK OUT
AT LOUFEST

Once upon a time—the "dark days," as referred to by serious music fans—our town didn't have one of those ginormous, multi-day, outdoor music festivals, the kind where one admission price gets you shows from a wide variety of big-name touring acts. Then along came LouFest to change all that; in fact, it raised the bar. Not only has the Forest Park–based festival brought the Flaming Lips, Jeff Tweedy, Alejandro Escovedo, and Carolina Chocolate Drops to play, but it's also provided big-crowd exposure for some great local acts. And the scene has remained refreshingly friendly, easy to navigate, locally celebratory (the local food vendors are especially good), and kid-friendly, if that's important to you. Look for consecutive festivals to keep upping the ante.

September, Central Field in Forest Park, www.loufest.com

SEEK OUT
THE CLASSIC MAGIC

Nothing against the newish digs at the Magic House, but trust me on this: Kids will actually get a kick out of climbing the tucked-away stairs up to what now qualifies as the "old" part of the interactive children's museum, where a certain threadbare charm still captivates. Up in the garret rooms, the pneumatic tube, Bernoulli balls, shadow wall, multi-story slide, and the iconic Van de Graaff generator (a.k.a. the hair-raising metallic orb) delight. Weirdest find in the attic? A tiny side room with a kid-size table, tea set, and Raggedy Ann and Andy dolls and readers.

516 S. Kirkwood Rd., 314-822-8900, www.magichouse.org

STROLL THE COBBLESTONES
IN HISTORIC ST. CHARLES

Main Street St. Charles aims squarely at the domesticated lady of a certain age, with its charming shops specializing in home décor, collectibles, teapots, Christmas ornaments, and baubles. Even if that's not you, though, it's a pleasant afternoon admiring the intact, historic business district, popping into the old-fashioned ice cream and candy shops, or settling in with a fresh beer at Trailhead Brewing Company. And there is real history to be found: Both Missouri's first state capitol and the Lewis & Clark Boat House and Nature Center will appeal to buffs.

www.historicstcharles.com

FETCH SOME FUN
AT MARDI GRAS

One of Soulard Mardi Gras' best events goes to the dogs, just as it should, on the day of the Barkus Pet Parade and Wiener Dog Derby, each February or March. Bring your well-behaved (and, if you must, well-costumed) pup or parrot out to stroll the streets in her finery, or just come along to gawk at the getups some patient pets will wear. And by all means catch at least one heat of the Dachshund dash, proof that anyone can develop that champion spirit, even if you're built more along the "low and slow" model.

314-771-5110, www.mardigrasinc.com

PARADE WITH A PURPOSE
FOR ANNIE MALONE

This town loves a parade! The May Day Parade, a 100-plus-year tradition that's intertwined with the African-American community here and across the state, is among the most joyous and entertaining. With floats, marching bands, dance, and step crews, the parade is a showcase and benefit for the Annie Malone Children and Family Service Center, a longstanding center for social services, educational programming, and advocacy for abused, neglected, and abandoned kids. Long held in the historic Ville neighborhood, its fans followed the parade when it moved to the more visible downtown route; a friendlier crowd you'd be hard-pressed to find.

May, starts at 20th & Market Sts., 314-531-0120, www.anniemalone.com

PLAY BOCCE BALL
ON THE HILL

The city boasts a tight-knit and intact ethnic neighborhood in the Hill, and you can work off your Italian dinner (see Dinner on the Hill, page 62) with a match of bocce ball at Milo's Bocce Garden. Unless you come from generations of players who've passed down their techniques to you, skip Monday–Thursday nights after 6 p.m. (league play). Open play welcomes all comers, though, and happens daily from 11 a.m. to 6 p.m., Friday and Saturday from 11 a.m. to 10:30 p.m. If you don't know your pallino from a Pabst, find a friendly old-timer to coach you on the finer points.

5201 Wilson Ave., 314-776-0468, www.milosboccegarden.com

More Local Lore

A handful of niche collections, open to the public, can shed further light on our history. At the Lutheran Church–Missouri Synod's International Center, a museum dedicated to preserving and sharing the history of Lutheranism in America, exhibits examine everything from the denomination's heritage and growth to its proliferation in our area. The Mercantile Library, the oldest library west of the Mississippi, is a trove of documents, artifacts, and art related to Westward Expansion and St. Louis history and prehistory. And the St. Louis Soccer Hall of Fame preserves the stories and memorabilia of the sport's parks, heroes, leagues, and highlights.

Concordia Historical Institute Museum
(Lutheran museum)
1333 S. Kirkwood Rd., 314-505-7900,
www.lutheranhistory.org

Mercantile Library
7606 Natural Bridge Rd. (at UMSL), 314-516-7248,
www.umsl.edu/mercantile

St. Louis Soccer Hall of Fame
5247 Fyler Ave., 314-781-8493,
www.eteamz.com/stlsoccerhalloffame

UNEARTH RECENT
MISSOURI HISTORY

Get a fascinating glimpse into the postwar decades in St. Louis, with exhibits examining suburban growth and land use patterns, playgrounds and neighborhood identity, civil rights protests and sit-ins, the role of professional baseball in the city's community life, significant writers and musicians from the area, and more topics in the Missouri History Museum's Reflections Gallery. Plenty of hands-on exhibits make this an especially kid-friendly corner.

5700 Lindell Blvd., 314-746-4599, www.mohistory.org

DRINK MISSOURI WINE

At a Missouri winery, of course: whether you enjoy the sweet stuff that built our historic viticultural district's early reputation, or you want to partake of award-winning Nortons, Chambourcins, Chardonels and other dry varietals, choose a reputable local vineyard and let them educate your palate.

Several wineries delivering a
reliably pleasant experience include:

Chandler Hill Winery
with a handsome indoor tasting room
and expansive patio
596 Defiance Rd.,
Defiance, 636-798-2675,
www.chandlerhillvineyards.com

Chaumette Winery
hilltop location, complete with gourmet dining and
overnight villas, in the rolling hills of Ste. Genevieve
24345 State Route WW, 573-747-1000,
www.chaumette.com

Stone Hill Winery
the granddaddy in historic Hermann, with tours
available of the arched-stone cellars, the state-of-the-
art production facility and tasting room
1110 Stone Hill Highway, 800-909-WINE,
www.stonehillwinery.com

RIDE ON
AT THE MOONLIGHT RAMBLE

A fifty-year tradition in the streets of St. Louis, the Moonlight Ramble is a massive nighttime bike ride along boulevards and byways that are closed to traffic, complete with costumes, entertainment, and general merriment under August's full moon. Bring the kids, wear a helmet, light your bike, and enjoy St. Louis in a whole new way.

August, 314-613-7966, www.moonlightramble.com

CELEBRATE THE SEASON
AT THE OLD COURTHOUSE

Holiday majesty doesn't get much more handsome digs than the rotunda of the historic Old Courthouse, in the shadow of the Arch. Typically starting the day after Thanksgiving, a revolving cast of invited performers—everything from brass quintets to children's choirs—offers free noontime concerts of Christmas and other holiday music. Singalong caroling in the authentic Victorian décor can't help but warm the heart.

11 N. 4th St., 314-655-1614, www.coreofdiscovery.com

Tip:

Spend the extra $2 per person for the children in your group to spend an hour inside Creation Station, a fun, hands-on space where they can play, dress up, craft, crawl, and generally unwind. It's air-conditioned, which on hot days will be well worth a few bucks for the adults, too. The Station, however, is closed to the public on weekends, to allow for private parties.

GET MOVING
AT THE MUSEUM OF TRANSPORTATION

The Museum of Transportation exerts an almost physical pull on both transportation-obsessed schoolkids and their Baby Boom-or-older grandfathers. You can see it in their eyes, as they wander the outdoor tracks loaded with historic locomotives, trolley cars, and streetcars, or inside showrooms displaying classic cars and aircraft. More than seventy locomotives, many the sole surviving examples of their type, are on display, but what will really move you are the streetcar and miniature train rides.

Auto buffs will enjoy the 1901 St. Louis Motor Carriage automobile, produced in 1901; the Bobby Darin custom "Dream Car," built in 1960; a 1963 Chrysler Turbine Car, the only operational model on public display in the world; and other interesting cars and trucks. For the landlocked, clambering about the decks of the *H.T. Pott* tugboat moored out front will provide plenty of fun.

3015 Barrett Station Rd., 314-965-6212,
www.transportmuseumassociation.org

GET UNDERGROUND
ON A CAVE TOUR

Get this: Missouri is sometimes known as "the cave state." No lie! There are 6,300 known and surveyed caves, and at least one (Meramec Caverns) where a recording of Kate Smith singing "God Bless America" warbles out at a critical point in the tour. For your spelunking excursion, we recommend two underground wonders at Onondaga Cave State Park, about eighty-five miles southwest of the city. Onondaga Cave itself offers an easy, under-one-mile stroll along paved walkways, with electric lighting and a tour guide (April 15–October 16, between 10 a.m. and 4 p.m.). Take it up a notch with a lantern tour of Cathedral Cave, a bit longer and more strenuous (May 15–September 15, with a more limited daily schedule; call for exact times). Either way, your old friends stalagmites, stalactites, and many other formations will be there.

7556 Highway H, Leasburg, 573-245-6576,
www.mostateparks.com/park/onondaga-cave-state-park

GO BIRD-WATCHING
ON OPENING DAY

The street party to end all street parties, Opening Day for Cardinals baseball season is practically a sanctioned day to play hooky. Make sure you're wearing red, so you'll blend into the crowds of office workers, schoolkids, and far-flung fans visiting their holy site. The constituents of Cardinal Nation mass in and around Kiener Plaza, where food, music, beer, Clydesdales, and general frivolity form a protective bubble around all who enter.

Early April, www.cardinals.com

GET STARSTRUCK
AT THE PLANETARIUM

Hearken back to 1962, when the space race was in full heat and President Kennedy promised a moon landing before decade's end. The following year, with the construction of the James S. McDonnell Planetarium at the Saint Louis Science Center, our town boasted one of only eleven large planetariums in the United States. Ours has the additional distinction of having been designed by renowned architect Gyo Obata. Its distinctive curvature is now a cherished civic icon. Step inside to experience the current night sky (minus the distraction of city lights), brush up on your constellations, or envision eclipses and meteor showers.

In Forest Park, near Clayton Ave. and Faulkner Dr., 314-289-4400, www.slsc.org

KNOW YOUR RIVER

For a great overview of both the cultural and historical importance of the Big Muddy, to the actual logistics of modern management of a very busy commercial waterway, trek to the Melvin Price Locks & Dam, and the National Great Rivers Museum. Tour interactive exhibits, try your hand at captaining a model barge, and hike up the eighty feet to overlook barges moving through the brilliant lock system. An education at any price . . . and for both, the price happens to be "free."

#1 Lock and Dam Way, East Alton, IL, 877-462-6979

NA ZDROWIE!

"To your health," a phrase that'll come in handy at the Polish Festival organized in the fall by the members of the Polish Falcons Nest 45, a fraternal organization that maintains a stately mansion HQ in North St. Louis. Prepare to polka, of course, and also enjoy some fine home cooking, beer, music, and the unstoppable pride of the Poles.

September 2013, St. Louis Ave., 314-421-9614

Want to explore more cultures with a presence in the metro area? Check out the St. Nicholas Greek Festival (Labor Day Weekend), Italian Fest in Collinsville (September), and Deutsch Country Days in October.

Greek Festival
4967 Forest Park Blvd., 314-361-6924,
www.sngoc.org

Italian Fest
221 W. Main St., Collinsville, IL, 618-344-2884,
www.italianfest.net

Deutsch Country Days
18055 State Highway O, Marthasville,
636-433-5669, www.deutschcountrydays.org

EXPERIENCE
PUMPKINLAND

City slickers and lil cowpokes alike are welcome here, with the October transformation of Thies Farm into Pumpkinland, complete with corn mazes, wagon rides, barnyard animals, corn cannons, crafts, face-painting, and free-range fun in the vast pumpkin-powered play area. And, of course, you'll leave with the perfect pumpkin.

4215 N. Hanley Rd., 314-428-9878, and 3120 Creve Coeur Mill Rd. South, 314-469-7559, www.thiesfarm.com

FAIRE THEE WELL
AT THE ST. LOUIS RENAISSANCE FAIRE

Get a visceral understanding of life in a sixteenth-century village, as represented through this annual festival re-enacting the song, dance, jousting, shopping, crafts, and entertainment of the era. Volunteer villagers take on the roles of peasants, nobility, knights, and ne'er-do-wells, and a special Kids' Kingdom teaches more about the customs of the time. It's a colorful spectacle that goes far beyond the giant turkey leg concession stand. The scavenger hunt will keep the young ones busy for hours. Weekends from mid-May to June.

Rotary Park in Foristell, 636-928-4141, www.renstl.org

WATCH SPRING EXPLODE
AT PURINA FARMS

Spring hasn't sprung until your wee lambs have held onto a squirming piglet, or stroked a downy chick, or milked a cow, or gotten their snapshot taken with Peter Cottontail; in short, spring really starts at Purina Farms. The annual Springtime Village extravaganza cries out for visits from family groups of all ages, and like so many good things in St. Louis, it's free (reservations required).

Last two weeks of March, days and times vary, 314-982-3232, 38 miles west of St. Louis on Highway MM in Gray Summit, www.purinafarms.com

Tip:

During Springtime Village or any other visit, the dog agility and trick shows (held two to three times a day) are a don't-miss. Nothing amazes and amuses like canines hell-bent on getting that Frisbee, even if it means a long leap into the splash pool. Frequent breed shows are a great way to meet up with every pup from Afghan Hounds to Yorkies.

CRUISE THE RIVER

For the best views of the downtown skyline, you've got to get a little distance, say, from the deck of a replica steamboat as it takes a one-hour sightseeing tour, offered several times daily for most of the year. Or put a different twist on it with one of the popular nighttime blues cruises, featuring live music from stellar local musicians, drinks and dancing, and the bright lights of the big city.

50 S. Leonor K. Sullivan Blvd., 877-982-1410, www.gatewayarch.com

WATCH THE WORLD
AT THE ST. LOUIS
INTERNATIONAL FILM FEST

Having one of those "woe is us/flyover territory" moments? Snap out of it fast at the St. Louis International Film Festival, which takes over screens throughout town for two weeks in November. The best in shorts, features, documentaries, and experimental film from around the world are accessed as easily as falling off a log and into a plush theater seat. It's also an excellent venue for showcasing the best in homegrown talent. Panels, discussions, and parties round out the schedule, and volunteers are always needed . . . and rewarded.

Presented by Cinema St. Louis, 314-289-4151, www.cinemastlouis.org

Tip:

Three miles north of downtown, just past the Merchants Bridge, stop at the Mary Meachum Freedom Crossing, the state's first documented site on the Underground Railroad, named for a free woman of color who accompanied a group of runaway slaves seeking passage to Illinois in 1855.

BIKE
THE RIVERFRONT TRAIL

Set out on two wheels to enjoy the best of city cycling, along eleven paved miles hugging the Mississippi River from just north of the Arch, at the Laclede Power Center, to the Old Chain of Rocks Bridge, an impressive bike/pedestrian span across to Illinois. Light industrial uses and natural elements combine to create an unforgettable juxtaposition of the wild and the urban; it's not uncommon to spot wild turkeys along the trail, in season.

Laclede Power Center parking at Leonor K. Sullivan Blvd. and Biddle St., one mile north of the Arch, 314-436-1324, www.confluencegreenway.org

EAT LEBANESE
WITH THE LORD

One of those "hidden restaurants" that flies right below the radar, the Wednesday buffet line at St. Raymond's Maronite Cathedral attracts a weekly mix of parishioners, politicians, exiles from nearby downtown offices, and more. The Lebanese specialties, cooked up by a crew of ladies (and a few gents) from "cafeteria central casting," include authentic kibbi, spinach pie, lentils and rice, and a lavish table of desserts. Bring cash or checkbook.

931 Lebanon Dr., 314-621-0056

ROLL THUNDER, OLD-SCHOOL
AT SARATOGA

Saratoga Lanes, in the bowling business since 1916, delightfully combines the improbable (a second-story location? Really? For a bowling alley?) and the familiar (a no-frills, retro-before-retro-was-cool setup) to create a space the whole gang (or family!) will love. Shoot pool while you wait your turn, drink beer while you shoot pool . . . the possibilities are enticing.

2725 Sutton Blvd., 314-645-5308, www.saratogalanes.com

LET THE MUSIC PLAY
AT POWELL HALL

You likely already know we have a world-class symphony orchestra, and yet that hasn't been enough to lure you out of the house and into Powell Hall, or it hasn't in a while? Perhaps one of these special events will. Lately, the St. Louis Symphony has taken to playing live scores along with big-screen projections of flicks like *The Matrix*, *The Wizard of Oz*, and *Pirates of the Caribbean*, to name a few. Want to hear full orchestral oomph behind some of your favorite pop music? Check out concerts devoted to the music of Queen, the Beatles, Whitney Houston, and others. And get your young ones acculturated early, with the terrific one-hour Family Concert matinees designed to engage the kiddos and let them experience live symphonic music without sky-high expectations for complete silence and stillness.

718 N. Grand Blvd., 314-533-2500, www.stlsymphony.org

Tip:

Bribe the short set with sweets after the family matinee: both City Diner and the Fountain on Locust are within easy distance for a post-concert milkshake or other treat.

HIKE THE GLADES
AT SHAW NATURE RESERVE

Take in the prairie and marvel at the springtime return of life to the woodlands. These landscapes reveal themselves within the nearly 2,500-acre Shaw Nature Reserve, at the juncture of several of the Midwest's diverse habitats. Spectacular wildlife viewing opportunities, plus trails overlooking the Meramec River, make every season Shaw season.

Highway 100 and I-44, Gray Summit, 636-451-3512,
www.shawnature.org

SEE A SHOW
AT THE SHELDON

Renowned far and wide for its acoustics (to say nothing of its handsome, wood-paneled stage and rich stained glass), the Sheldon is a perfect concert experience. Best bang for the buck is the "Notes from Home" series, featuring local standouts on select weeknights for a low price.

3648 Washington Blvd., 314-533-9900, www.thesheldon.org

Tip:

Rental chairs are available if lounging on your own blanket is not your thing. Arrive between 5:30 and 8:00 for first-come, first-served options. You should aim to arrive by 6:30 anyway, as that's the kickoff time for the nightly Green Show, featuring jugglers, singers, and a short preview of the show.

TAKE YOUR MAMA FOR SOME DRAMA
AT THE SHAKESPEARE FESTIVAL

Or perhaps one of the comedies? Depending on the year, the Shakespeare Festival of St. Louis might be performing any of the playwright's timeless works, but whether you lean more towards the tragic or comedic, the theatergoer in you will be utterly enchanted by the outing. Free outdoor productions in a sylvan glade in Forest Park (the east side of Art Hill, now dubbed "Shakespeare Glen"), on a summer night with a loaf of bread, a jug of wine, and the company of your fellow citizens: Bardic bliss.

In Forest Park, May-June, 314-531-9800, www.sfstl.com

SWOON FOR
A SUMMER NIGHT

Make like old times and point your vehicle east, for a double feature at the Skyview Drive-In. You pay, you park, you watch a feature film or two on the big screen under the stars. One upgrade that has taken place since days of yore: Instead of a speaker slung over each car's window, the movie's sound is now transmitted via FM radio. Tickets are cash only (about $10/person, with two kids free with each paying adult), and bringing your own food and drink is allowed, so plan ahead. Want to bring lawn chairs, blankets, a bucket of chicken, and your dog? No problem. It's the rare treat that lives up to its fun factor in your memory: luckily, this is one.

5700 North Belt West, Belleville, IL, 618-233-4400,
www.skyview-drive-in.com

SHOP THE STALLS
OF SOULARD MARKET

Any place in business since 1779 must be doing something right: in this case, bringing together vendors of everything from fresh, organic produce to knockoff designer sunglasses. The mini-donuts alone will keep you moving while you ponder meats, cheeses, spices, baked goods . . . and maybe that pet bunny you've been considering. The real bargain, though? All this people-watching is free. Saturday morning is the best bet.

730 Carroll St., 314-622-4180, www.soulardmarket.com

SETTLE A GRUDGE MATCH
AT SOUTH BROADWAY ATHLETIC CLUB

You'll feel like you're in on the reckoning of a grudge match, from your seat, ringside, at the South Broadway Athletic Club's monthly local wrestling lineup. Outrageous characters (Gorgeous Gary Jackson, the Big Texan, Moondog Rover, and Shorty Biggs are but a handful of the regulars), girlfights, chair-breaking—all are included with the price of admission. A bit like low-rent WWE, if you can imagine such a thing. Keep the cheap beer flowing to help you get in the spirit. You may even find yourself taking a fan photo with your favorite after the evening's athletics.

2301 S. 7th St., 314-776-4833, www.saintlouiswrestling.com

TAKE A TWIRL
AT STEINBERG RINK

Under the twinkling lights, tucked beneath the urban bustle of the Central West End, Steinberg Rink provides the backdrop for an almost-storybook winter experience: outdoor ice skating in one of the nation's largest public parks. And you! Gliding gracefully on your rental skates, belly warmed by hot cocoa, hand warmed by the hand of your beloved, heart warmed by a city that would provide you this moment.

In Forest Park, 400 Jefferson Dr., 314-367-7465,
www.steinbergskatingrink.com

FILL UP
THE MARKET BASKET

For the most complete farmers' market experience, the weekly Tower Grove Farmers' Market can't be beat. Some of the region's most conscientious and innovative growers, food producers, and even craftspeople bring their wares to the central pavilion area of Tower Grove Park for your shopping (and snacking) pleasure. Figs, tomatoes, wild honey, proper British scones, corn, pumpkins, apples, grass-fed beef, spring lamb, rainbow chard, fresh pasta . . . the list is kind of making me hungry right now. Throw in the free yoga, great live music, and adjacent kiddie pool and playgrounds, and you've got a perfect summer Saturday. Saturdays from May to October, 8 a.m. to noon.

In Tower Grove Park, Center Cross Dr., www.tgmarket.org

Here in the heartland, great growers' markets abound. Enjoy any (or all!) of the following, in season.

Ferguson Farmers' Market

Saturdays, May-October, 20 S. Florissant Rd., 314-324-4298, www.fergmarket.com

Maplewood Farmers' Market

Wednesday afternoons April-October (once-monthly winter markets on Saturdays), 314-241-2337, www.schlaflyfarmersmarket.com

Kirkwood Farmers' Market

Daily (Sunday and seasonal hours vary by vendor), 150 E. Argonne Dr., 314-822-0084, www.kirkwoodjunction.com

Land of Goshen Community Market

Saturdays, mid-May to mid-October, downtown Edwardsville, IL, 618-307-6045, www.goshenmarket.org

Clayton Farmers' Market

Saturdays, May-November, 8282 Forsyth Blvd., 314-913-6632, www.claytonfarmersmarket.com

North City Farmers' Market

Saturdays, June-October, North 14th St. and St. Louis Ave., 314-241-5031, www.northcityfarmersmarket.blogspot.com

Tip:

Of the slate of festivities, on both sides, leading up to the big game, chili fests on Wednesday night may be the most well attended. Each school offers a bevy of entrants, from amateur and class chilis to school board and professional chef varieties. The winners of the respective "professional" categories go head-to-head to be crowned the winner of the coveted Chili Bowl.

REVEL IN RIVALRY
ON TURKEY DAY

The "oldest Thanksgiving Day football rivalry west of the Mississippi" carries on, as it has every Turkey Day since 1907, between the Kirkwood Pioneers and the Webster Groves Statesmen. The game is at high noon on the appointed Thursday, with the 400-pound Frisco Bell awarded to the winner, and the consolation prize—the Centennial brown jug—goes to the losing school. Families have had generations on the field and in the stands, so get your ticket early if you're planning to carpetbag in for the main event.

The game's location alternates, with Kirkwood High School hosting odd-numbered years, and Webster Groves High School taking evens.

SHARE A SECRET
AT UNION STATION

Take someone trustworthy to the northern entrance of Union Station's Grand Hall, and position yourselves with backs to each other across the expanse. The sweet nothings (or juicy some-things) you utter to the Whispering Arch will travel right over.

1820 Market St., 314-231-1234, www.stlouisunionstation.com

CHILL OUT
AT VENICE CAFE

Leave your cares (and credit cards) behind, and enter the parallel relax-iverse that is the patio at the Venice Café. Part hippie hangout, part music venue, part psychedelic mosaic party HQ, the Venice is a staple of St. Louis nightlife. You can tell a lot about a bar by how many folks in the industry are willing to spend their downtime there . . . and here, the answer is, "a lot." The bathrooms—even the bathrooms!—have more personality than some entire other establishments. Sample the jerk chicken, kebabs, and drinks; come by for a band or open mic show; and see if you don't lose track of time.

1903 Pestalozzi St., 314-772-5994, www.thevenicecafe.com

GET UP ON THE ROOF
AT VIN DE SET

For as much as St. Louisans love to dine and drink alfresco, it's surprising more restaurateurs haven't followed the lead of Vin de Set and put a classy establishment overlooking some scenic part of town. Ponder the mysteries of that and other phenomena while enjoying Chef Ivy Magruder's French-inspired dishes and some amazing beverages on the all-season patio, or in the soaring space inside.

2017 Chouteau Ave., 314-241-8989, www.vindeset.com

DIG UP NEW TUNES
AT VINTAGE VINYL

You don't have to be a hard-core crate digger to get into the groove at Vintage Vinyl. Go in, start with something you already know, and before long, the handmade signage, the multiple listening booths, and the live-mixed, in-store soundtrack will lead you down the rabbit hole.

6610 Delmar Blvd., 314-721-4096, www.vintagevinyl.com

ALL ABOARD!
WABASH FRISCO AND PACIFIC RAILROAD

Want to blow your toddler's mind? If your wee ones (or for that matter, your father-in-law) loves everything about trains, a half-hour ride in the woods aboard an honest-to-goodness steam engine—albeit a 12-gauge one, meaning it's akin to sitting on a moving ottoman—will give them plenty to ooh and ahh over. Plan for a short wait in line, the hiss and pop of the wood-fired engine, the shrill whistle echoing in the air, and the scenic riverbank views you'll all remember.

109 Grand Ave., Glencoe, 636-587-3538, www.wfprr.com

CHANNEL YOUR
INNER ARCHITECT

The Frank Lloyd Wright House in Ebsworth Park (that's FLWHEP to you) provides a pristine example of the aesthetic of the renowned architect, right down to the original furniture and fabrics he designed for the home's interior. Tours of the Kirkwood site by appointment only, Wednesday to Sunday.

120 N. Ballas Rd., 314-822-8359, www.ebsworthpark.org

WEDNESDAY EVENING CONCERTS
IN THE WHITAKER MUSIC FESTIVAL AT MISSOURI BOTANICAL GARDEN

Right in line with all the rest of our fabulous free attractions, this summer series—from June to August—has fast become a place to hang out with thousands of your nearest and dearest pals. Enjoy a picnic dinner, a bottle or two of wine, and some of our town's best musicians in a variety of genres, under the stars and amidst the blooming glory of the Garden.

Music starts at 7:30 p.m.

4344 Shaw Blvd., 314-577-5100,
www.missouribotanicalgarden.org

Bringing the kids?

Arrive at 5 p.m., when admission to the grounds is free, and your sprouts can run themselves ragged in the Children's Garden until 7 p.m.

WADDLE THE ZOO

The ever-entertaining king and gentoo penguins waddle on their wintertime Sunday walkabouts (weather permitting, of course . . . only in this case, the colder, the better!) The birds are loosed from their interior habitat to parade from the nearby gift shop to Penguin & Puffin Coast's entrance, with enchanted visitors snapping photos and marching alongside. Sundays at 2 p.m. from early December through early February.

One Government Dr., 314-781-0900, www.stlzoo.org

SUGGESTED ITINERARIES

THE CLASSIC STL TRIFECTA

Anheuser-Busch Tour, 3
Gateway Arch, 52
Cardinals Opening Day, 91

HITS FOR MUSIC LOVERS

BB's, 8
Chuck Berry Concert, 10
Bluesweek, 12
Compton Heights Concert Band, 32
Jazz at the Bistro, 61
Scott Joplin State Historic Site/Ragtime Rendezvous, 68-69
Loufest, 76
St. Louis Symphony Orchestra, 106
Vintage Vinyl, 123
Whitaker Music Festival, 126

DATE NIGHT

Casa Loma Ballroom, 21
Ferris Wheel Atop City Museum, 30
Riverboat Cruise, 100
St. Louis International Film Festival, 101
Saratoga Lanes, 105
Ice Skating at Steinberg Rink, 115

SPORTY SPOTS

Arch Madness, 4

Busch Stadium Tour, 16

Sailing at Creve Coeur Lake, 35

Gateway Cup Bicycle Races, 53

Moonlight Ramble, 86

Cardinals Opening Day, 91

Riverfront Trail, 103

South Broadway Athletic Club, 114

Kirkwood–Webster Groves Turkey Day Game, 119

THE GREAT OUTDOORS

The Confluence, 34

Float Trip, 47

Lone Elk Park/World Bird Sanctuary, 74-75

Caving at Onondaga State Park, 90

EAST SIDE ADVENTURES

Cahokia Mounds, 17

Eckert's, 44

Eagle-watching at the Audubon Center at Riverlands, 42

Bobby's Frozen Custard, 50

Great River Road, 57

Skyview Drive-In, 112

FOODIE FAVORITES

Brewers Heritage Festival, 15

Eating Along Cherokee Street, 27

DiGregorio's Market, 37

Donuts, 41

Slinger, 43

Festival of Nations, 46

Frozen Custard, 51

Missouri Wineries, 84

St. Raymond's, 104

Tower Grove Farmers' Market, 116

Vin de Set, 122

FUN WITH KIDS

Balloon Glow, 7

Best of Missouri Market, 11

Carousel/Butterfly House/Faust Park Playground/Hayride, 22-23, 45

Circus Flora, 29

City Museum, 30

Citygarden, 31

Grant's Farm, 54

Magic House, 77

Museum of Transportation, 89

Pumpkinland, 96

Wabash Frisco and Pacific Railroad, 124

OFF THE BEATEN PATH

Bellefontaine Cemetery Tour, 9

World Chess Hall of Fame, 28

Joe's Café, 67

Lemp Mansion Tour, 72

The Loop Ice Carnival, 73

South Broadway Athletic Club, 114

ACTIVITIES
BY SEASON

There's always fun to be had in St. Louis, but some events and activities are best enjoyed, or only happen, at specific times of year. Below are some ideas to keep you busy no matter the season.

WINTER

Sledding on Art Hill, 5
Christmas Lights on Candy Cane Lane, 19
March Morpho Mania at the Butterfly House, 22
Eagle-watching, 42
Lenten Fish Fries, 48
The Loop Ice Carnival, 73
Mardi Gras Pet Parade and Wiener Dog Races, 79
Holiday Caroling at the Old Courthouse, 87
Ice Skating at Steinberg Rink, 115

SPRING

World War II Weekend at Jefferson Barracks, 66
Mother's Day Art Fair at Laumeier Sculpture Park, 71
May Day Parade, 80
Springtime Village at Purina Farms, 98
Hiking at Shaw Nature Reserve, 108

SUMMER

Bluesweek, 12

Summer Solstice at Cahokia Mounds, 17

Circus Flora, 29

Splashing at Citygarden, 31

Festival of Nations, 46

Float Trip, 47

Moonlight Ramble, 86

Caving, 90

Renaissance Faire, 97

Shakespeare Festival, 111

Soulard Market on a Saturday Morning, 113

Whitaker Music Festival, 126

FALL

Balloon Glow, 7

Best of Missouri Market/Historic Shaw Art Fair, 11

Apple-picking at Eckert's, 44

Hayrides at Faust Park, 45

Gateway Cup Bicycle Races, 53

Foliage Drive on the Great River Road, 57

Halloween in the Central West End, 60

Japanese Festival, 65

Pumpkinland at Thies Farm, 96

St. Louis International Film Festival, 101

Turkey Day Football Game, 119

Wabash Frisco and Pacific Railroad Ride, 124

INDEX

4 Hands Brewing, 2

Akers Ferry, 47

Angel Avenue, 19

Anheuser-Busch, 3

Annie Malone Parade, 80

Annie's, 50-51

Apop, 27

Arch Madness, 4

Art Hill, 5

Assembly Series, 6

Audubon Center at Riverlands, 42

Balloon Glow, 7

BB's Jazz, Blues and Soups, 8

Barkus Pet Parade, 79

Bearcat Getaway, 47

Bellefontaine Cemetery, 9

Berry, Chuck, 10

Best of Missouri Market, 11

Blueberry Hill, 10

Bluesweek, 12

Boat House, 14

Bocce Ball, 81

Bobby's, 50-51

Brewers Heritage Festival, 15

Busch Stadium, 16

Butterfly House, 22

Cahokia Mounds, 17

Calvary Cemetery, 9

Campbell House, 20

Candy Cane Lane, 19

Cardinals Baseball, 16, 91

Carl's Drive-In, 36

Carousel, 22-23

Casa Loma Ballroom, 21

Cassilly, Bob, 30

Cathedral Basilica, 24

Cathedral Cave, 90

Central Library, 26

Central West End, 28, 60, 69, 115

Chandler Hill Winery, 85

Chaumette Winery, 85

Cherokee Street, 21, 27

Chess Club, 28

Christman, Bill, 67

Circus Flora, 29

City Diner, 107

City Museum, 30

Citygarden, 31

Civil Life Brewing Co., 2

Clydesdales, 3, 55, 91

Columbia Bottom Conservation Area, 34

Compton Heights Band, 32

Compton Hill Water Tower, 33

Concordia Historical Institute Museum, 82

Confluence, 34

Creve Coeur Lake, 35

Crown Candy, 36

Deutsch Country Days, 95

DiGregorio's, 37, 62

Dogtown St. Patrick's Day Parade, 38-39

Dominic's, 62-63

Donut Drive-In, 40-41

Donuts, 40-41, 113

Duke Bakery, 40-41

Dressel's Pub, 69

Eagle-watching, 42, 75

Eat-Rite, 43

Ebsworth Park, 125

Eckert's, 44

Eddie's Donuts, 40-41

Faust Park, 22-23, 45

Festival of Nations, 46

Firecracker Press, The, 27

First State Capitol, 78

Fish Fry, 48-49

Float Trips, 47

Flowers to the P

Forest 44 Canoe Re

Forest Park, 5, 7, 14, 2

Fountain on Locust, 107

Francis Park, 32

Fritz's, 50-51

Frozen Custard, 50-51

Gateway Arch, 52

Gateway Cup, 53

Gooolll, 27

Graham Chapel, 6

Grant's Farm, 54-55

Great Forest Park Balloon Race, 7

Great River Road, 56-57

Greek Festival, 95

Griot Museum of Black History, 58

Gus' Pretzels, 59

Halloween in Central West End, 60

Hill, the, 37, 53, 62, 81

I Scream Cakes, 27

Italian Festival, 95

Japanese Festival, 65

Jazz at the Bistro, 61

Jefferson Barracks, 66

Joe's Café, 67

Joplin, Scott, 68-69

Kirkwood Pioneers, 119

Laumeier Sculpture Park, 71

La Vallesana, 27

Moonlight Ramble, 86

Museum of Transportation, 88-89

ational Great Rivers Museum, 93

Fashion Donuts, 40-41

Chain of Rocks Bridge, 42, 103

Courthouse, 87

ndaga Cave, 90

pening Day, 91

Pat's Bar & Grill, 39

Main Street on St. Charles, 78

Pere Marquette State Park, 56

Mardi Gras, 79

Piasa Bird, 57

Mary Meachum Freedom Crossing, 102

Planetarium, 92

May Day Parade, 80

Polish Festival, 94

Melvin Price Locks & Dam, 93

Powell Hall, 29, 106

Meramec Caverns, 90

Pumpkinland, 96

Meramec River, 47, 108

Purina Farms, 98

Mercantile Library, 82

Ragtime Rendezvous, 69

Milo's, 81

Renaissance Faire, 97

Mississippi River, 34, 42, 57, 103

Riverboat Cruise, 100

Missouri Botanical Garden, 11, 65, 126

Riverfront Trail, 103

St. Cecilia, 48-49

Missouri History Museum, 83

St. Charles, 78

Missouri River, 34

Saint Louis Art Museum, 5

Missouri Valley Conference, 4

Saint Louis Brewers Heritage Festival, 15

Missouri Wine, 84

St. Louis Curio Shoppe, 27

Mr. Wizard's, 50-51

St. Louis International Film Fest, 101

Mo Moderne, 27

Saint Louis Science Center, 92
St. Louis Soccer Hall of Fame, 82
St. Louis Symphony, 106
Saint Louis Zoo, 128
St. Peter, 48-49
St. Pius V, 48-49
St. Raymond's, 104
Saratoga Lanes, 105
Scott Joplin House, 68
Shakespeare Festival, 111
Shaw Art Fair, 11
Shaw Nature Reserve, 108
Sheldon, 109
Siete Luminarias, 27
Skyview Drive-In, 112
Slinger, 43
Snow Flake Street, 19
Soulard Market, 113
South Broadway Athletic Club, 114
Springtime Village, 98-99
Steinberg Rink, 115
Stone Hill Winery, 85
Strange Donuts, 40-41
Stylehouse, 27
Ted Drewes, 50-51
Thies Farm, 96
Tower Grove Farmers' Market, 116
Tower Grove Park, 32, 46, 116

Turkey Day Game, 119
Union Station, 120
Urban Chestnut Brewing
   Company, 2
Venice Café, 121
Vin de Set, 122
Vintage Vinyl, 123
Wabash Frisco and Pacific
   Railroad, 124
Washington University, 6
Webster Groves Statesmen, 119
Whistle Stop, 50-51
Whitaker Music Festival, 126
World Bird Sanctuary, 75
World Chess Hall of Fame, 28
World's Fair Donuts, 40-41
Wright, Frank Lloyd, 125
Zia's, 62-63